THE GENSHAI EFFECT

THE GENSHAI EFFECT

Genshai - (pronounced Gen-shy)
"Never treat anyone in a manner which makes them
feel small, including yourself."

Let us plant a seed.

On any given day, the human experience is one riddled with emotions. We all have our high points, our low points, points of stagnation or trepidation, pain, love, gratitude, and a pondering of our purpose and our self-worth. Depending on the 'nature' of the day, there is an effect on how we feel and treat ourselves and others.

We co-exist while we are here.

Let's make the most of it by giving, living and mastering Genshai.

The word Genshai is a word that awakens us. It reminds us to check in with ourselves and do our best to right what is wrong within and to utilize our innate excellence to impact the exterior forces that can seize us if we are not equipped to release their grip.

Genshai encourages us to demonstrate compassion and love for others in the moments of great spirit and grace, and even in the cases when we may feel challenged.

Embracing Genshai gives us permission to forgive and be kind to ourselves. Self- love is inherent, but not always innate. It becomes a practice. It makes us realize that it is just fine to ask, "What about me?" and, "What may I do for you?"

On our paths, which will be many, we can look within to explore and discover what compels us to be who we are in a given moment and across time. Genshai compels us to understand that it matters how we choose to show up or be in our world.

In life, we play to our strengths, but sometimes we do not even know the strength that we have. We don't know until something affects us and we go deep inside. It may be buried until that seed is nurtured and cracked. Our greatness has been embedded in us our entire lives, but until we tap into it, how will we ever know the extent of it?

Welcome to The Genshai Effect.

Brevity...From the Authors

Many of us are practical people. We have to be in a chaotic world, though sometimes it takes time to get to this place. What if we misstep – if chosen on purpose or otherwise – yet then realize, it is with the wisdom that comes from those experiences that shines a light on the way forward. Don't always believe your own press – that which is inside your head or that which others might convey. Be your own story.

Compiling a small, yet significant book, that is chalked full of ideas, thoughts, and ways of thinking beyond what we currently even know can be seen as strange or uncomfortable to a reader. However, we were evidently destined to do this and to do all we can to create The Genshai Effect.

We discovered that once we stopped pushing, it just started pulling us. We discovered it is amazing when you let go what actually appears. We realized that in respecting our own innate excellence, we were actually able to step into it – or at least start to....and continue.

So, our desire is to give you thoughts, deeds, actions, vision, and love. To every Genshai Warrior....Enjoy! And, give, live and master Genshai!

ENVISION THE GENSHAI EFFECT

Envision **Giving Genshai** in the realm of how we treat ourselves and contribute in our communities, as parents, in businesses and in developing the growth of our future leaders. The resulting culture becomes a habitat for acceptance, challenge, thinking big and working to improve together.

Envision **Living Genshai** and how that will make you feel in any interaction. Just repeating the word in your mind as you have encounters every day will impact how you are seen and how you see others. Imagine living Genshai in a business environment Imagine this in your home, with those you love and who you want to love themselves.

Envision **Mastering Genshai** as a lifelong pursuit. There are so many milestones as we go through the stages of the life experience. Some are so wonderful and some are tragic. The way we choose to perceive what happens to us or that which we make happen...well, that is a matter of shifting our gaze to the potential in the experience and stepping into our excellence.

So, our desire is to give you thoughts, deeds, actions, vision, and love. To every Genshai Warrior....Enjoy! And, give, live and master Genshai!

It's your call or decision. Genshai is a foundation for making the more informed call. You may not always get it right. No one does. But, at least you will know the difference.

Throughout the ages, humanity has experienced changes and shifts. How we choose to show up each day, however, is simple. Living, Giving and Mastering Genshai is our possibility together.

Will you walk with us to activate The Genshai Effect?

It's time for the seed to grow.

GENSHAI

Genshai is an ancient sacred word that means—

"Never treat another person in a manner that would make them feel small – including yourself."

You begin with **giving** to yourself first because you cannot give what you do not have.

Next, you implement by **living**, meaning you embody the meaning of Genshai in your everyday interactions with others and with yourself.

Then, you practice **mastering** throughout each day, which leads to realizing your excellence. A master never stops learning and once we learn we want to give back which takes us to the beginning of the cycle.

GIVING GENSHAI

*Envision **Giving** Genshai in the realm of how we interact and contribute in our communities, as parents, businesses and to the growth of our future leaders. The resulting culture becomes a habitat for acceptance, challenge, thinking big and working to improve together.*

There is an old adage that you must give to yourself before having the ability to give to others. Too often, we think it is inappropriate to simply take good care of ourselves – our hearts, bodies and our minds. Selflessness, is doing just that or we are ill-equipped to be and do more for others.

Have you ever felt as if you are a victim?

Have you been the person that belittled yourself or others?

Now, knowing the meaning of the word, Genshai, how does the word and its meaning make you feel? It **IS** your possibility, our possibility....and it **IS** an opportunity.

Go into the inquiry of having a world that gives Genshai.

Putting yourself first provides an unselfish nature. Fulfill yourself. What are the stories you tell yourself? Likely, it is a mixed bag. There will be the times when you give yourself the 'atta boy or atta girl' pat on the back, and deservingly so. Create more of those times. It is innate within you to do so.

There will also be the times when you step into the gutter. You know those times. We've all had them, often many of them. It truly is okay to feel badly on occasion. It is part of human nature and sometimes life just bites us. The advice though, is not to stay there for too long. The way you get out of the doldrums is to do something good whether that is for yourself or for another person. Take a first step to emerge and you will experience The Genshai Effect.

There are a lot of adages that we learn through the years: Treat your neighbor as you wish to be treated yourself; Say 'please, thank you and your welcome', Turn the other cheek. Yet, until now, most of us have not been familiar with one word that pulls it all together:

GIVING GENSHAI

What about you?

Why is it that so many of us have trouble saying how great we are? Do not get this wrong. Not many like a bragger. However, it needs to become much more than okay to indicate your goodness, your greatness, your talents, your skills, your contributions. Now, of course, there is a way to do this that resonate with others rather than repel them.

What is the way?

Well, you start with some humility, not over-stating or exaggerating, making relevant your remarks in the context in which you are speaking them, and making dang sure you are not boasting to make yourself superior and helping your insecurities go away. This requires awareness. And, it requires giving pause before opening your mouth. Ask, does this help or hinder this relationship, proposition or my reputation. The above is not meant to preach, but on the road to giving, living and mastering Genshai, the idea is that you are aware of your effect on others.

It **IS** a Genshai Effect if someone walks away feeling better than when you found them.

It **IS** a Genshai Effect if you shared a story about your-self that makes someone even more pleased to be in your presence.

We are not saying you cannot cry, go on a rant, be audacious or step out on the limb of silliness....just choose wisely the people you do this with and be clear on your intention. If it is pure do it. If it is not, don't. Simple. Live with the audacity to be "YOU", and with the humble nature of realizing no one, including you, is perfect.   Make a mistake. Make an apology. Get on with it.

It's about You.

You breathe the air you breathe.

You can create the space for others to accept and acknowledge their innate self. We are not exempt from the stuff of life. It makes us who we are. And, though we traverse the path within the body and mind we have been given, it is never done alone. Even if a person tries to 'do it' alone...it is an impossibility. Love goes a very long way. People or a person....will be there whether you request that interference, input, insight or intelligence. This YOU, you must eventually come to know. YOU will have many who choose to be 'this' for you. And, you will choose to be 'this' for many. Keep your mind open so you are open to all possibilities. Be open to all things and attached to none.

So...YOU. What we impart is this:

You are so much more than okay.

YOU ARE INFINITE.

This is the essence of NEVER TREATING YOURSELF IN A MANNER WHICH MAKES YOU FEEL SMALL! Hold Yourself in Your Own Excellence.

ACTIVATE GIVING GENSHAI

- In your moments of crisis or as champion.....
  just say and think Genshai. Recall its meaning
  and exemplify it. This will not go unnoticed
  and in a split second, you have created The
  Genshai Effect.

- Experience nature. We often tell ourselves
  we do not have time. Make time for yourself.
  If only minutes of appreciating your
  surroundings, be aware.

- It helps to have a touchstone. Carry the
  Genshai coin with you. Its power is in its
  meaning. It is a reminder of the possible
  and of your excellence in any moment of
  decision, response, reaction or remembrance.

- Pass a Genshai coin on as you continue to
  activate Giving Genshai. Giving the coin holds
  everyone in their own excellence.

  First coin – Giving to yourself first. You cannot
  give what you do not have.

  Second coin – Give this coin to the one person
  who positively impacted your life and share the
  story of how.

ACTIVATE GIVING GENSHAI

- Consider your SELF (and remember "What bout me"). Fill in the blank:

I wish _____

I want _____

I accept _____

I love _____

I will _____

I must _____

I choose _____

I am...

_____

_____

_____

_____

_____

LIVING GENSHAI

*Envision **Living** Genshai in a home and business environment and imagine the implications to the true bottom line of how life is lived and loved. Think people, profit, prosperity and posterity.*

The trajectory of life is never a straight line. It ebbs and flows and sometimes, we have the gift of it calming for just a bit. The costant in it is your choice. There may not be a better feeling than to feel good about who you are and what you do and how you might make another person simply smile. There is something precious in that. Precious is such a great word....or world. Utilize the thinking and the words that instigate that feeling in yourself and in others.

We are never a victim...except to the thoughts we have. Will you choose to overcome those thoughts? They will happen. No doubt. And, to address and overcome them, it helps to make another person simply feel good. You do not have to know that person personally.

And, those that you are close to, well, isn't it simply your possibility to help them over a hump, a bump in the road, create a nicer day, illicit a laugh, calm the worries....we could go on....and we should, because that is your possibility in EVERY day. Not sure it gets better than knowing someone is better because of your presence.

If there is a person in existence that has not been put out, peeved, irked, angered, or completely fatigued by another...please point us in that direction. We might have to summit a few mountains to find the Sherpa.

If there is a person that has not intimidated, criticized, hurt, blamed or shamed you personally, well, you are in fortunate stead, as it would be a rarity to go through life without that happening. People are people, and we suppose what that really means is that we are flawed. From the time of creation, this has been true. No one is exempt.

The course of life is to realize that it is a course. Consider it as a giant blue marble of a classroom and a broader field of the universe to explore. We might 'figure it out' problem by problem, though we will not 'figure it out' in its totality. The miracle of life is the curiosity of what is next and why it is so – whatever IT is.

Let's acknowledge that when people behave in a certain manner there is a root cause for it. If a person is being a 'not so nice' person to you or others, try delaying your judgment. Who knows what that person is going through? Does he or she know what you are facing in the moment? Probably not. Behavior and words are typically the result of stress, worry, patterns, insecurity and so many more descriptors.

It does not mean that poor behavior is okay, though with Genshai, you first deliver the benefit of the doubt and you often try to shift that person's mental state to help them see their existence and their interactions in a more positive way – even if they do not realize you actually just did that.

Is it a matter of patience for you? Abso-freak-ing-lutely!

And, it is also a skill. Develop it.

So why wax on in this philosophical strain? (and it is a strain)   The answer? Because we can or we must. We are always searching for meaning and answers. And, unless you are on an island, there are people you will have to either interact with or with whom to contend.

How will you traverse that landscape or those waters or that mountain or that wilderness or in your own home, at work and even at play? It's true....there may be trial by fire, but the winds of change, spirit, and time will see you through. Flow does return and you will be grounded once again.

Our belief is not that when the going gets tough, the tough get tougher. That can help at times and is situational. Maybe, there can also be an inclination for getting softer in asking for help, shedding a tear, going into nature, being quiet for a few minutes, journaling....and in the elements of it, realizing what works for YOU.

A STORY:

A Genshai Experience in Bangladesh

As for how the authors of this book choose to live....we are willing to travel anywhere in the world without fear (or too much of it anyway) so that we can bear witness to those who may be seen as different than ourselves.

We traveled together to Bangladesh. Upon arriving Dhaka, the capital, we were unaware that 17,000 people had gathered at the US Embassy to protest a negative portrayal of them in a movie trailer. We were blissfully unaware as we took in this incredibly busy city with rickshaws and buses and traffic and so many people. It was amazing and overwhelming to experience.

On our trip we visited the Mangrove Forest.

We were transferred to a houseboat and then set out to sea. Each morning at dawn, we would board a small craft that allowed us to enter canals and see the flora and fauna (snake, monitor lizard, owls, egret, and let us not forget butterflies and lady bugs, etc.) We were flanked by 'tiger guards' who are there not only to protect the habitat, but to protect us from Bengal Tigers.

One morning, we nearly missed the most magnificent sunrise of our lives.

It was a rare time we had phone coverage and we had our heads down. Yes, texting. We looked up and saw the essence of our Creation, and did not look down again on that trip. It was an awakening to raise our eyes and bask in that glory.

At one point, we docked at a rickety ladder and crossed a birch bridge where a community of people were dressed in their most beautiful attire to welcome us. They proudly showed us their Tiger Shrine and then put on a 'concert' for us in a hut. No electricity, but the atmosphere was pure energy. They had never seen an American. They looked upon us with curiosity, as we did them. That show of dancing little girls, singing among the townspeople, and even a tiger attack (with costumed men of course), rivaled anything we had seen, as it was such a true stage. The performances were a reflection of their lives and an appreciation for ours. Though we did not speak the same language, there was the language of love. We will never forget the faces and the feelings as we parted, knowing we would not see one another again in this lifetime.

The next day we returned to port and had a 2-hour drive to the local airport. In route, we began to see men in their faith-based garments and then heard chants coming from a distance. The only words we could make out were USA and America. We had entered a riot zone. There were about 1000 men gathered in the 'town square' and they were not happy. Without radio, TV or newspapers, it was the true definition of viral marketing, as word of the supposed movie trailer attacking their beliefs had made its way to this remote place.

They did not realize two Americans were actually in their midst. We were asked to move to the middle of the van and we got stuck between two buses. Our guides went quiet, not informing us of what was being said. We were not sure what to do next. Lance began to text his beloved daughters. Kristin observed the gathering from the window. We went within...figuratively and literally. Men looked in at us with angry faces, but it was as if a shroud was placed over us. They were on each side of the van and it is not as if we blended with our looks or our attire. We were different. Yet, we remained safe, and humbled.

As we alas drove outside of the town, we were very quiet and then it dawned on us how we, as people, use the word 'they' so very often. However, have we put a face with that amorphous 'they'? Do we know someone, anyone who represents what we might despise or criticize?

When we say 'the world' is against me or us, who makes up the world? People! Generalizations and stereotypes can make us hateful and ignorant if we buy into them without the knowledge and wisdom of truly putting faces and hearts with an actual person. Take a moment to shift a belief system that culminates in the potential of humankind interacting with one another, first to learn and then to grow the seed of goodness and Genshai together.

In the quiet following the experience, we realized the reason for our trip. It was to return love. And, that is what we did. The next day, we went to what would be our equivalent of a Ronald McDonald House and we served the children and their parents lunch. We did not communicate in words, but in deeds. We broke bread together, shared smiles and hugs, took pictures and saw pain and also healing. The fathers may have been part of that gathering or protestors, and yet when we each put a face to our different nations and beliefs, there was an imparting of love and of goodwill.

Most people are amazing....if we choose to see – truly see – them from the inside of their hearts. As you live, give and master Genshai, do your very best to love others, no matter what.

This will activate the Genshai Effect.

Activate Living Genshai

- Each day acknowledge another for who he or she is in your life. Make a conscious effort to do so.
- Remind yourself that you are responsible for stepping into our excellence regardless of circumstances. Keep your Genshai coin front and center as your touchstone.
- It does become simpler if you realize, embrace and practice the principle definition of Genshai - "Never treat anyone in a manner which makes them feel small, including yourself."

- Who needs you?_____

- What do you need?_____

- What love will you be?_____

- What do you need to learn and practice?

  _____

Give it a whirl and see what happens.

MASTERING GENSHAI

*Envision **Mastering** Genshai as a lifelong pursuit.
There are so many milestones as we go through the
stages of the life experience. Some are so wonderful
and some are tragic. The way we choose to perceive
what happens to us or that which we make happen...
Well, that is a matter of shifting our gaze to the
potential in the experience.*

STEPPING INTO YOUR OWN EXCELLENCE

Stepping into your own excellence is not about
material riches. Stepping into your excellence is about
the riches in how you define the meaning of the loveli-
ness of your existence.

What is it that makes you feel more than good?
Who is it? How will you invest your days? What are
the outcomes that make a life well lived, or.... lived
well? How will you choose to treat yourself? How will
you choose to treat others?

EXCELLENCE **IS** A CHOICE

It is true that we all have individual gifts. However, it does not benefit us to covet that which we are not intended to embody. One person is a writer. One person is a visionary. One person is an athlete, another is a scholar, a dancer, a parent, a speaker or even a star. That list could be long, because humanity was designed to be diverse. How boring if it were not.

Being true to you, is stepping into your excellence. When you embrace yourself instead of compare yourself... there is a freedom in thought, deed, gesture and countenance... and a musicality that resonates with hearts, especially your own.

No doubt, there will always be external circumstances that hinder our thoughts, minds, our bodies, our families and our days. This may test our resolve, but has no power to defeat us – certainly not if we believe in our own excellence and that of those we decide to work, live or play with.

There will be noise from sources of media, people, ideas and environment. AND (not but).....how will you embrace the facts or the fiction or the event or the fantasy you create in the purview of your world? You cannot always believe your own press.

Rise above it. Own your excellence.

Sometimes. Often times. Always.

There is more of a solution in the questions we ask of ourselves. In life's many moments, we need to be able to adjust and engage ourselves in the recognition that 'this' (whatever this is) is happening or can happen. The reality, albeit harsh, is that we do not have access to tomorrow. So, the question is, what do you do with today? With every day? It is not as if every day has to be regimented. You have to do what you have to do. Though, give yourself a moment. Several if possible.

As you get ready for the day, drive to work, drop off the kids, step into the elements.....breathe. Sift through what is important, what are your priorities, how will you determine your day? The day and experiences are certainly going to happen. You might as well be as ready as possible within.

It is so very easy to get caught up. If there is a person on any planet that does not have this happen....oh, please, let him or her step forth. We have responsibility and inclination and needs and wants and a purpose and oh geez....that's a lot of head and heart space. Acknowledge that this happens.

We get into that spiral because that's just what we do. We can be the most learned, experienced, spiritual, and whatever....and still, we happen to be people with thoughts or beliefs or prayers or fears. We are a collection of misfits and wants and want nots and misunderstandings and misgivings and...and....and...   And, we are WE. You are YOU.

Mastering Genshai is lifelong....and every moment is yours.

There will be times when we lose our perception. This is literal and figurative. In a digital age, our technology may go caput at what we feel is the least opportune of times. In reality, perhaps it is intended – so that we raise our countenance to encounter a sunrise. Our reception of all that can be seen in the goodness of our surroundings is in large part dependent on our willingness to see it – and each other. This holds true in what and how and who we need to show up for ourselves.

We each have much to look forward to – day by day.

ACTIVATE MASTERING GENSHAI

- Who have you told they have meaning in your life? If you have not done so lately, do it now, this minute. The outcome will:

Create a wave -
who is your water? _____

Stir an ember -
who is your fire? _____

Draw a breath –
who is your wind? _____

Ground you in excellence –
who is your earth? _____

Elevate grace? -
Who is your spirit? _____

- Who told you recently that you have meaning in their life? Surrender to this. It does not make you vulnerable. It makes you more powerful to step into your excellence.

- Love.   Love you. Love people. Love difference. Love...absolute.

- Say it or think it out loud. Deep breathe in and deep breathe out.

Mastering Genshai is a lifetime of being this for one another.
It is the Genshai Effect.
The culminating Effect of being good to ourselves

WIND - FREEDOM

Your Genshai Wind Warriors liberate your thoughts and ideas and give them flight. They lift you and breathe into your dreams.

FIRE - IGNITE

Your Genshai Fire Warriors challenge you to be passionate about how you show up in the world and serve as a light within it. They kindle your possibilities

WATER - FLOWING

Your Genshai Water Warriors connect you to the ebb and flow of the experiences in your heart. They help you relate to others and exemplify compassion.

SPIRIT - GRACE

Your Genshai Spirit Warriors elevate your awareness of the nature and goodness of humanity. They bring out the divine in your soul.

EARTH - GROUNDING

Your Genshai Earth Warriors bring you stability through practical advice, acceptance and reliability. They escort you through life's changes.

THE GENSHAI EFFECT

By now, you have an understanding that life, whatever it looks like for you, is not a straight line. No one gets it right all of the time. No one. When you do get it right in a day or a moment, then simply smile and know that when the 'what's next' comes...you get it, got it or have it.

From beginning to end, it is yours to own.

Once you start the Genshai Effect....it is the perpetual effect you have on yourself and others. The intrigue is that you want that effect for yourself, your sons and daughters, your mom and dad, a neighbor, your communities and nations. In us, is created the insatiable desire to understand or simply accept who we are and who are the others among us.

There is simplicity of the vastness of Genshai. Keep encompassing it. It affects not only humans, but the nature around us. The animals. The trees. What do you notice in the world around you? Open your eyes and truly see. Take and make time to see the lady bug that hovers gently on your arm, the butterfly that flutters effortlessly through the breeze, the puppy thumping his or her tail in greeting, your child's laugh.

To be awakened is to awake to our world's beauty and all that we give and receive within it. When you see a rainbow, a waterfall, a wildfire, an eagle flying, an earthquake, a cloud formation, an embrace, an ocean swell, a snowcapped mountain peak, a brilliant sunset, a tear rolling on a cheek, a survivor or words of a saint or sauvant.....what is the effect? On you? On others? On Us? There is an energy around it that flows because that is the lifeblood of who you are. You do not sit back and let whatever 'It is' happen... you forge toward it. You charge the hill. You yell at the top of your lungs. You embrace it for the unknown. You part the mist.....because it is within you to do so. And, you realize that whatever may lie ahead is yours to captivate, lay captive to, and to simply own.....

No one does this for you, but they do it with you.

Never are you alone on this endeavor. Always, you have footprints ahead, beside and behind. You are gifted....open the gift. The wrapping is yours to define. Elaborate or not. Yes or no. Sad or happy. You must claim it as 'mine'.

The pathway is intense and interesting and problematic at times. We have people get in our way and we get in our own way. Shift your gaze. If in doubt look up.

Realize....this....this...this...is up to you and to a collective 'us'. Breathe into it. Do not accept everything. Create what is needed. Put aside stress and worry as best you can. Ask for what you need. Listen to others – and mostly to the quiet. Be quiet. Let quiet be and you will hear.

Let's meet each other where we are. There is no other place anyway. And, let's lead ourselves to where we need to be. Be. Just be.

Activate Giving, Living and Mastering Genshai.... for you and for others, that provides an essence of.... well, you fill in the blank.........

Your Genshai Effect is for you to explore and embrace and embark.
The result is for us to discover The Genshai Effect together.

To give, live and master Genshai.....creates an effect within yourself. Only you will know what that is, though you WILL know it.

It is.....The Genshai Effect.

AND NOW...

"Never treat anyone in a manner that makes them feel small,

including yourself."

Consider this a formal invitation to be a Genshai Warrior

in creating the

GENSHAI EFFECT

Much love. Big love.

GENSHAI

Text "Genshai" to 801.436.6089 to receive your personal invitation. For more information, visit www.Genshai.com and connect with us on our social media platforms. @living_genshai

We welcome your participation in sharing coins, podcasts, events, blogs, courses and much more. We also welcome your Genshai stories at www.Genshai.com/media

ABOUT THE AUTHORS

Lance Schiffman

Lance Schiffman's endeavors read like a roll call: philanthropist, entrepreneur, adventurer, investor, author, speaker, consultant, coach, humanitarian, advisor, and closest to his heart, he is a father to three beautiful girls. He started his first business before age ten, and by age 20 he owned an apartment complex and gas station. This led to his interests in commercial and residential real estate. With keen interest in participating in others' success, he invests financial and intellectual capital in ventures which have forward thinking and resilient leadership.

Lance utilizes his business and life experiences to identify the elements of wonder and uses this as a platform to educate others on how to play full out and create a more engaged world. He believes what we cultivate has a ripple effect to economies, relationships, innovation, productivity, contribution, personal significance, and the intelligence of peace and a new horizon for how we live together in the world.

An avid outdoorsman, Lance climbed Mount Kilimanjaro and Mount Elbrus. He loves endurance sports such as Triathlons (Ironman), DOXA and Cycling. He runs the mountain on which he lives in Summit, Utah each day, encountering moose and wildlife. Nature and his faith are his guides.

Kristin Andress

If you rest on your laurels for long in life or business, Kristin Andress is bound to ask you, "How is that working for you?" She is on a perpetual quest to create the What's Next.

Kristin began her career in corporate America and after the life of a road warrior, she exited and took two years off to write books, and become an entrepreneur with focus on bettering the world in which we live. Her best day is a day she delivers a bold idea. Over the years she has worked with high profile individuals, authors, speakers, and business owners. She believes everyone is accessible...if you have an offer that reflects pure intention and authenticity.

Kristin's is the co-author of Imagine Being in a Life you Love. She is a contributing author in Leading Women: 20 Influential Women Share Their Secrets to Leadership, Business and Life. She released an allegory titled, Be Good For Goodness Sake She is also the author of the children's book A Walk in the Park. Her next quest will be traveling and writing around the world, reflecting the principles of Genshai. She currently lives in sunny San Diego.

Made in the USA
Las Vegas, NV
26 May 2024

90372125R00024